ROME

NICOLA BARBER

WORLD ALMANAC® LIBRARY

Please visit our web site at: www.worldalmanaclibrary.com
For a free color catalog describing World Almanac® Library's list of high-quality books
and multimedia programs, call 1-800-848-2928 (USA) or 1-800-387-3178 (Canada).
World Almanac® Library's fax: (414) 332-3567.

Library of Congress Cataloging-in-Publication Data

Barber, Nicola.
    Rome / by Nicola Barber.
        p. cm. — (Great cities of the world)
    Includes bibliographical references and index.
    ISBN 0-8368-5040-8 (lib. bdg.)
    ISBN 0-8368-5200-1 (softcover)
    1. Rome (Italy)—Juvenile literature. I. Title. II. Series.
    DG804.2.B37   2004
    945'.632—dc22   2004047977

First published in 2005 by
World Almanac® Library
330 West Olive Street, Suite 100
Milwaukee, WI 53212 USA

Copyright © 2005 by World Almanac® Library.

Produced by Discovery Books
Editor: Kathryn Walker
Series designers: Laurie Shock, Keith Williams
Designer and page production: Keith Williams
Photo researcher: Rachel Tisdale
Diagrams: Keith Williams
Maps: Stefan Chabluk
World Almanac® Library editorial direction: Mark J. Sachner
World Almanac® Library editor: Gini Holland
World Almanac® Library art direction: Tammy West
World Almanac® Library graphic design: Scott M. Krall
World Almanac® Library production: Jessica Morris

Photo credits: AKG Images: p. 16; AKG Images/Erich Lessing: p. 12; AKG Images/Nimatallah: p. 9; AKG Images/Pirozzi:
pp. 13, 36; Axiom/Peter M. Wilson: p. 33; Corbis: pp. 10, 14, 21, 39; Corbis/Vittoriano Rastelli: pp. 34, 43; Corbis/Sandro
Vannini: pp. 41, 42; Corbis Sygma/Fabian Cavallos: p. 35; Corbis Sygma/Gianni Giansanti: p. 22; Corbis Sygma/Alberto
Pizzoli: pp. 37, 38; Chris Fairclough: pp. 4, 17, 18, 20, 24, 27, 29, 30; Hutchison/Trevor Page: pp. 26, 28; James Davis
Worldwide: p. 8; Still Pictures/Peter Schickert: cover and title page; Trip/Helene Rogers: p. 25; Trip/Bob Turner: p. 32

**Cover caption: One of Rome's favorite meeting places, the Spanish Steps is a famous tourist attraction. Built in the
eighteenth century, the steps link the Piazza di Spagna with the church of Trinità dei Monti.**

Printed in the United States of America

1 2 3 4 5 6 7 8 9 08 07 06 05 04

Contents

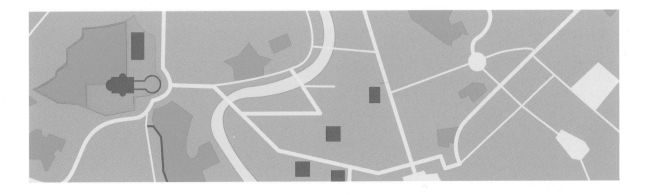

Introduction

R ome is the capital of Italy. A beautiful and astonishing city, it is crammed full of ancient monuments, galleries, museums, and great architecture. Over the centuries, Rome has inspired artists, poets, and writers from many countries, and its long, rich history has earned it the name the

◄ *A view over the city from the Gianicolo Hill. The mixture of architectural styles of the many monuments and churches bear witness to Rome's long history.*

"Eternal City." Today it is a busy, modern city, home to international organizations such as the United Nations and major banks. It also serves as the seat of the Italian government.

In ancient times, Rome was once the capital of the vast Ancient Roman Empire, which covered much of the Mediterranean region and western Europe. In the years that followed the empire's collapse, in the fifth century, the city suffered invasions, looting, and general neglect. Revival came during the Renaissance of the fifteenth and sixteenth centuries, when Europeans' renewed interest in learning and the arts made Rome again a center of culture and learning. During this period and the century that followed, Rome acquired many beautiful buildings and works of art and the city became great once more. When Italy became a unified country in 1871, Rome was made its capital.

The history of Rome can be seen all over the city in the form of ancient ruins, beautiful churches, palaces, statues, fountains, and squares. Not surprisingly, the city is a huge tourist attraction, and every year millions of people come from all over the world to walk its cobbled streets.

Rome contains within it the Vatican City, the center of the Roman Catholic Church. The Vatican City has been an independent state within Rome since the Lateran Treaty of 1929. Rome is therefore a center for pilgrimage and in the Jubilee Year (Roman Catholic Holy Year) of 2000, millions of pilgrims, celebrating two thousand years of

CITY FACTS

Rome
Capital of Italy
Founded: 753 B.C.
Area (Commune of Rome):
580 square miles
(1,500 square kilometers)
Population: 2.6 million
Population Density:
4,483 people per square mile
(1,740 people per square km)

Christianity, joined the regular flow of tourists in the Eternal City. In preparation for that special year, Romans gave their city a massive spring cleaning, and undertook many major public works projects, such as road building. Both tourists and residents have benefited from this concentrated effort to improve the city.

The Vatican City

The Vatican City is the smallest independent state in the world, covering only 0.17 square miles (0.44 square kilometers). It has its own postal system, newspaper, telephone network, banking

"Rome, a lifetime is not enough."

—Popular saying about the many attractions of the city.

Commune of Rome

city area of Rome

extent of the commune of Rome

Olympic Stadium

Vatican City   Centro Storico

Leonardo da Vinci International Airport (Fiumicino)

Catacombs

Cinecittà

Tiber River

EUR

Ciampino International Airport

Ostia Antica

Palazzo dello Sport

N

Tyrrhenian Sea

miles
0   5
0   5
kilometers

▲ Rome's centro storico (historical center) lies at the heart of the city of Rome. The city and a large outlying area together form an administrative unit know as the commune of Rome.

City Walls

In modern Rome, the area known as the centro storico *(historical center) marks the extent of the ancient city. From earliest times, this area was surrounded by a wall for protection from invaders. In A.D. 271, the Roman emperor Aurelian decided to improve existing defenses by building a new wall, 12 miles (19 km) long. Parts of this wall still stand today, along with several entrance gates into the centro storico. The Vatican City is also surrounded by a high wall, erected in the ninth century under the direction of Pope Leo IV as a defense against invaders.*

system, and radio station. A high wall surrounds the Vatican and its gates are locked at midnight. It is protected by the Swiss Guard, young Catholic men from Switzerland who are responsible for the pope's safety. The Swiss Guard was first brought to the Vatican in 1506 by Pope Julius II, who had been impressed by their skill in battle.

The Tiber

Ancient Rome was founded alongside the Tiber (Tevere), a river which has its source far to the north in the Appenine hills near Arezzo in Tuscany. A small island in the center of the river, Isola Tiberina, offered the only crossing place for people of ancient times, and a settlement developed around this crossing. The river flows on to enter the Tyrrhenian Sea at Ostia, passing Ostia Antica on its way. This was ancient Rome's seaport, but the harbor has long since filled with silt. Today, the Lido di Ostia is the nearest beach resort to Rome. The Tiber used to flood regularly, causing huge amounts of damage. However, since the late nineteenth century, the embankments along the river have been built up to prevent the flood waters from spilling over.

Seven Hills

According to tradition, Rome was built on seven hills that lie on the east bank of the river: the Aventine, Caelian, Capitoline, Esquiline, Palatine, Quirinal, and Viminal. Today the city spreads far beyond these

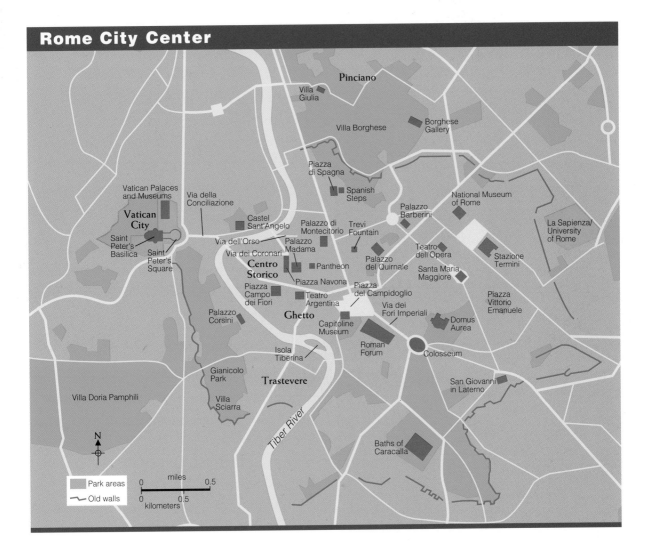

Rome City Center

Pinciano

Villa Giulia

Villa Borghese

Borghese Gallery

Piazza di Spagna

Vatican Palaces and Museums

Via della Conciliazione

Spanish Steps

National Museum of Rome

Palazzo Barberini

La Sapienza/ University of Rome

Vatican City

Castel Sant'Angelo

Palazzo di Montecitorio

Trevi Fountain

Saint Peter's Basilica

Via dell'Orso

Palazzo Madama

Teatro dell'Opera

Via dei Coronari

Saint Peter's Square

Centro Storico

Pantheon

Palazzo del Quirinale

Stazione Termini

Santa Maria Maggiore

Piazza Navona

Piazza del Campidoglio

Piazza Campo dei Fiori

Teatro Argentina

Via dei Fori Imperiali

Piazza Vittorio Emanuele

Palazzo Corsini

Ghetto

Capitoline Museum

Domus Aurea

Isola Tiberina

Roman Forum

Colosseum

Gianicolo Park

Trastevere

San Giovanni in Laterno

Villa Doria Pamphili

Villa Sciarra

Tiber River

Baths of Caracalla

N

miles

0   0.5

Park areas

0   0.5
kilometers

Old walls

seven hills and includes other equally prominent hills such as the Pincio and the Gianicolo. The Vatican City stands on the Vatican Hill in the west of the city.

Climate

Spring and fall are the most pleasant times of year in Rome. The weather is usually warm and sunny, although there is the occasional heavy shower of rain. Summers are very hot, with temperatures up to 104°

▲ *The area within the city walls is packed with palaces, churches, monuments, parks, and ancient ruins. The walls were built in the third century A.D.*

Fahrenheit (40° Celsius). If they can, many Romans leave the city and head for the coast and hills during the hottest weeks. Winters can be cool and wet with heavy rain and an icy wind called the *tramontana*. Winter, however, also brings days of brilliant blue skies and sunshine.

CHAPTER 1

History of Rome

Although the true origins of Rome are not known, there is evidence of settlement dating from the ninth century B.C. According to the ancient Roman historian Livy, however, Rome was founded on April 21, 753 B.C. by Romulus, and this is the date that is still celebrated as Rome's birthday. Livy's account was based on the myth of the twins, Romulus and Remus, sons of the war-god Mars, who were abandoned on the banks of the Tiber River. A she-wolf looked after the twins until they were rescued by a shepherd. When they grew up they founded a settlement but quarreled over who should rule it. Romulus eventually murdered his brother in order to become king.

In fact, the first historically documented king of Rome was an Etruscan, Tarquinius, who ruled from 616 B.C. The Etruscans were a tribe who lived in central Italy from the middle of the ninth century. They controlled Rome until 509 B.C., when they were overthrown by the Romans. Their overthrow marked the end of the kingdom of Rome and the start of the Roman Republic.

◀ *The Foro Romano (Roman Forum) was the heart of the vast Roman Empire. Located between the Capitoline and Palatine Hills, this was the city's business, political, civic, and social center, with a law court, government buildings, temples, and basilicas.*

The Roman Republic

The Romans appointed two officials, called consuls, to run the republic. The consuls were elected every year, and took advice from a council called the Senate. However, only members of the aristocratic "patrician" families were permitted to belong to the Senate or vote for the consuls. In 494 B.C., discontent among ordinary Romans, known as plebeians, boiled over. As a result, two representatives of the plebeians, called tribunes, were elected to the Senate. A code of law, called the Twelve Tables, was also drawn up to provide a legal framework for the republic.

Nero and the Domus Aurea

Emperor Nero ruled Rome from A.D. 54 until A.D. 68. In A.D. 64, a great fire destroyed much of the city. Although Nero was not in Rome when the fire started, rumors quickly spread, holding him responsible. Nevertheless, Nero embarked on a great rebuilding project, the centerpiece of which was his own palace, the Domus Aurea (Golden House). The palace was itself destroyed by fire in 104, but descriptions of its walls inlaid with precious stones, its dining hall with a slowly revolving roof, and its golden façade crowned with a huge golden statue of Nero, give us an idea of its lavishness. After twenty years of restoration work and further archaeological excavation, some of the rooms of the Domus Aurea (pictured right) have been reopened to the public.

"He found Rome in brick, and left it in marble."

—From the memoirs of Emperor Augustus, boasting of his transformation of Rome, c. A.D. 14.

Meanwhile, the Romans were busy bringing other tribes, including the Etruscans, under their control. Rome expanded as it became the center of an increasingly large empire. The Romans soon came into conflict with the other major power in the region—the Carthaginians, who controlled much of North Africa and Spain. The wars between the two, called the Punic Wars, ended in 146 B.C. when the Romans destroyed Carthage.

Imperial Rome

The last years of the Republic were marked by instability as different consuls struggled for power. In 44 B.C., Julius Caesar was proclaimed dictator for life, but one month later, on March 15, he was assassinated. The Roman Republic finally came to an end in 27 B.C., when Augustus became the first Roman emperor. The age of Augustus brought peace and a time of expansion. Drawing on the vast wealth of the Roman Empire, Augustus built and restored many buildings in the city. The population soared, reaching more than one million by the time of the emperor Trajan's reign (A.D. 98–117).

Early Christian Rome

During the reign of Tiberius (A.D. 14–37), a Jewish man was executed by crucifixion in a corner of the Roman Empire. This man was Jesus Christ, and his followers, called

▲ *Rome's famous landmark, the Colosseum, was built in A.D. 72 as a place of public entertainment. Here, Romans watched gladiators or prisoners fighting each other or wild animals to the death.*

Christians, began to spread word of his teachings. By the time the apostles Peter and Paul came to Rome, Christianity had already taken root in the city. The Roman authorities, however, were very suspicious of this new religion, and Christians were persecuted. Peter was crucified and Paul was beheaded, probably at some time between A.D. 64 and 69. Nevertheless, Christianity continued to flourish in Rome.

In 313, Emperor Constantine allowed Christians to worship freely in the city for the first time. He built many churches in Rome, including a huge basilica erected over the site of Saint Peter's tomb. It stood until the sixteenth century, when much of it was demolished to make way for the Saint Peter's Basilica that we see today in the Vatican City. The building of the first Saint Peter's, and other churches, ensured that Rome would become a center of Christian faith and pilgrimage.

End of Empire

While Christianity gained a hold in Rome, the Roman Empire was crumbling. From the third century A.D., the Romans found it increasingly difficult to control their vast empire, which included all countries surrounding the Mediterranean, parts of the Middle East, and present day England. In the fourth century, the empire was split in two. The eastern part became the mighty Byzantine Empire, with its capital at Constantinople (present-day Istanbul, Turkey). Compared to Constantinople, Rome became increasingly insignificant. The city was invaded and looted by two Germanic tribes, the Visigoths in 410 and the Vandals in 455. In 476, the Germanic general Odoacer deposed the boy emperor, Romulus Augustulus, ending the western part of the Roman Empire. Over the following century, Rome fell into ruin and decay. Its population dropped drastically as people fled its disease-infested streets.

During the sixth century, Pope Gregory I did much to establish Rome as the main Christian center in the West. Despite the power of the Roman Church, however, the city fell further into decay throughout the medieval period. Then, in 1309, Pope

"For the present I know not where to start, overwhelmed as I am by the wonder of so many things and by the greatness of my astonishment."

—Petrarch, Italian scholar and poet, describing his reactions to Rome, *Rerum familiarium,* c. 1350.

Clement V abandoned Rome and moved the papal residence to Avignon in France. It was not until 1377 that the pope returned to Rome. The French cardinals later elected a new pope to the Avignon seat, causing a division within the Catholic Church that lasted for more than forty years.

Renaissance Rome

With the election of Pope Martin V in 1417, the division within the Church came to an end. The papal residence was securely

San Giovanni in Laterano

San Giovanni (Saint John) in Laterano was one of the basilicas founded by Constantine in the fourth century and is the oldest Christian basilica in the city. Built on land once owned by the Laterani family, it contains the cathedra *—the official seat of the pope, who is also the bishop of Rome—and as a result was, and remains, Rome's cathedral. The basilica has been destroyed by fire twice and rebuilt several times. The Lateran Palace, next door to the basilica, was the home of the pope until 1309.*

back in Rome and the city remained under papal rule until 1870. Martin V began the process of restoring the filthy and crumbling city. This work was continued by Pope Nicholas V (1447–1455), who was determined to make Rome into a worthy home for the papacy. Nicholas restored churches and rebuilt the Vatican Palace, which became the residence of the pope. He brought the Renaissance painter Fra Angelico to work in the city and he founded the Vatican Library. He also planned the rebuilding of Saint Peter's, although work on it did not start until the following century.

▼ In 1508, Pope Julius II commissioned Michelangelo to paint the ceiling of the Sistene Chapel in the Vatican Palace. It took the artist four years of back-breaking work to complete this masterpiece.

"There are many splendid palaces, houses, tombs and temples . . . but all are in ruins."

—Alberto de' Alberti, visitor to Rome describing the city, 1444.

As Rome prospered once more, the papal court became a center for luxury and opulence. Great Renaissance architects and artists such as Donato Bramante, Raphael, and Michelangelo were brought to Rome to work on the new Saint Peter's and in the Vatican Palace. Pope Leo X (1513–1521), brought the papacy near to bankruptcy with his love of sumptuous banquets, hunting, and hawking.

Yet despite the construction and renovation of many churches and palaces,

and the pope's lavish lifestyle, Rome remained a medieval city for most of its inhabitants. Its streets were a maze of alleys and lanes, with small houses crammed together. Inside the crumbling city walls that remained from the glorious days of the Empire, people planted vines among the ruins. Wild boar and deer lived in patches of woods and wasteland around the city. Cattle, sheep, and goats wandered the filthy streets.

The Sack of Rome

During the sixteenth century, the two major powers in mainland Europe were France and Spain. When Pope Clement VII allied himself with France, Charles V of Spain sent troops to attack Rome. In 1527, a large army sacked the city, killing, burning, and destroying as they went. Pope Clement VII took refuge in Castel Sant'Angelo (Saint Angelo's Castle) and eventually gave in to his defeat.

The Counter-Reformation

Meanwhile, another force was attacking the power of the Church in Rome. In 1510, a German monk called Martin Luther came to Rome on business. He was appalled at the corruption of the Roman Catholic Church and seven years later launched an attack on

> "A desert of decay, sombre and desolate; and with a history in every stone that strews the ground."
>
> —Charles Dickens, English author, describing Rome, *Pictures from Italy*, 1846.

▲ Renaissance and Baroque buildings line the Piazza di Navona. In the foreground is Bernini's Fontana di Fiumi (Fountain of the Rivers), built in 1651.

the Church, calling for reform. His actions marked the start of the great sixteenth-century religious revolution, known as the Reformation, and the birth of the Protestant Church. Under Pope Paul III (1534–1549), Rome became the center of the Counter-Reformation, a reform movement within the Roman Catholic Church that sought to find answers to the charges of the reformers.

Artists and Writers in Rome

During the Baroque period, an era that lasted throughout the seventeenth century and for part of the eighteenth century, the wealth of the Catholic Church was used to erect numerous fine churches, fountains, and monuments in Rome. The two architects responsible for many of these structures were Gian Lorenzo Bernini and Francesco Borromini. Increasingly, the splendors of Rome attracted tourists, particularly artists and writers. They included the French artists Nicolas Poussin and Claude Lorraine, the English Romantic poets John Keats, Percy Bysshe Shelley, and Lord Byron, and American writers Nathaniel Hawthorne, Henry James, and Mark Twain.

◄ *The magnificent Trevi Fountain, completed in 1762, is a late example of the Baroque style and Rome's largest fountain. It is said that if you throw a coin into it, you will be sure to return to Rome.*

A New Country

In 1797, Rome was looted once again, this time by the French armies of Napoleon Bonaparte. Napoleon declared a new Roman Republic in 1798, but papal rule was restored in 1801. However, in 1808, Napoleon removed the pope and papal rule was not re-established until after Napoleon's defeat in 1814. This taste of liberty from papal rule encouraged the *Risorgimento* (Resurgence)—a movement for the unification of the many small states and kingdoms that existed in Italy. In 1861, the Kingdom of Italy was founded with its capital at Turin.

In 1871, after the unification of Italy was complete, Rome became its capital. The new king of Italy, Victor Emmanuel, moved into the Palazzo del Quirinale (Quirinal Palace)—previously the pope's summer residence—and the pope withdrew into the Vatican. The capital needed offices for the ministries of the new country and homes for the civil servants who were working in them. Therefore, a huge amount of building took place in Rome toward the end of the nineteenth century.

The Rise of Fascism

The Fascist movement started in the northern Italian city of Milan under the leadership of Benito Mussolini. The word "Fascism" comes from "fasces," referring to the rods that were carried by magistrates in ancient Rome as a symbol of authority. In 1922, Mussolini sent his troops, who dressed in black shirts, on a "March on Rome." Mussolini demanded complete power over the government, although the king remained as a figurehead.

Mussolini wanted to glorify Rome's ancient past and planned some ambitious building projects to sweep away the

"Either the government will be given to us or we shall seize it by marching on Rome!"

—Benito Mussolini, Italian dictator, speaking at a Fascist Congress in Naples, 1922.

15

▲ *The Fascists under the leadership of Benito Mussolini (pictured here at front of picture, second from right) march on Rome in October 1922.*

medieval parts of the city, but only a few of them were actually carried out. Among those projects that were built are the huge complex known as the EUR (*see box, page 17*) in the south of the city and two new avenues—the Via dei Fori Imperiali and the Via della Conciliazione. The Via della Conciliazione was named to celebrate the Lateran Treaty (known as the *Conciliazione* in Italian), which was agreed between the Italian government and the Vatican in 1929 and made the Vatican City into a separate state within Rome.

Open City

Mussolini, who allied Italy with Adolf Hitler's Nazi regime in Germany, took Italy into World War II, in 1940, when he felt confident of a German victory. By 1943, however, the Allies (the countries that fought against Germany and its allies) were poised to invade Italy. The Italian king had Mussolini arrested and Italian allegiance switched to the Allies. Adolf Hitler immediately ordered the German occupation of much of Italy, including Rome. In an effort to protect it against the destruction of war, Germany declared Rome an "open city"—a city not to be defended even if it was attacked. In fact, Rome suffered only one serious bombing raid from the Allies.

This was a dangerous time for the escaped Allied prisoners-of-war who were hiding in Rome and, because of the Nazi persecution of the Jewish people, for the city's large Jewish population. Many Roman residents risked their lives to help these people hide or escape. The end of the occupation of Rome came in 1944, and Mussolini was executed in the following year. In 1946, Italy voted to become a Republic once more. Then, in 1957, the Treaty of Rome created the European Economic Community (EEC), later known as the European Community (EC), with Italy as a founding member. This was an association of European countries working to create European economic unity.

The 1960s and 1970s in Rome were marked by student protests and terrorism. In 1973, thirty-two people were killed when Palestinian terrorists bombed a Pan Am office at Rome's Fiumicino Airport. In 1978, the former Italian prime minister Aldo Moro was kidnapped and murdered by a terrorist organization called the *Brigate Rosse* (Red Brigade).

Despite terrorism and widespread corruption at all levels of government and business, Rome, as Italy's capital, made much progress on improved trade and political union with Europe. In 1992, Italy and other EC members signed the Maastricht Treaty. With it, the EC became the European Union (EU), which strives to promote political, legal, and economic unity in Europe. Italy, like some other EU countries, now uses the euro instead of its old currency, the lira.

EUR

EUR stands for Esposizione Universale di Roma (Universal Exhibition of Rome). This was an international exhibition planned for 1942 to mark twenty years of Fascist rule in Italy, although it did not take place because of World War II. The EUR exhibition park was built south of Rome and was intended to form the impressive entrance to a new town that would extend to the coast at Ostia. In fact, only a few of the planned buildings were completed, notably the Palazzo della Civiltà del Lavaro, meaning "Palace of the Civilization of Labor" (pictured below). It acquired the nickname the "square Colosseum" because its arcades of windows echoed those of the ancient Roman landmark.

CHAPTER 2

People of Rome

Ancient Rome had the largest population of any city in the world at that time, yet Rome's population was reduced to just a few thousand during the medieval era. When Rome became capital of Italy in 1871, both Milan in the north and Naples in the south had larger populations. Today, Rome has the largest population of any Italian city. Every year, its resident population swells by the millions as tourists and pilgrims flood into the city.

Rome is home to a large number of immigrants—about one-fifth of the immigrant population of the whole of Italy live there. Immigrants in Rome come from all over the world, mainly from other parts of Europe and from Asia, with many others from Africa and the Americas. They are important to the Roman economy because they tend to do jobs that Italians are unwilling to take on.

"If you are at Rome live in the Roman style; if you are elsewhere live as they live elsewhere."

—Saint Ambrose, Italian bishop, philosopher, and author, fourth century.

◄ *Crowds gather at the Porta Portese flea market. The market is held on Sunday mornings along the Via Portuense on the east bank of the Tiber.*

Birth Rate

With the older residents (those aged sixty-five or more) outnumbering the young (those under fifteen years of age), Rome has what is known as an ageing population. This mirrors the situation in Italy as a whole. Italy has one of the lowest birth rates in the world—the rate of 1.19 children per woman is well under the the 2.1 needed to keep the population constant. The government has tried to address the problem with cash incentives for having children, subsidized childcare, and paid parental leave, yet many Italians still choose not to start a family.

▼ *A low birth rate combined with the fact that people today are living longer has created an "ageing population" in Italy, as seen in this chart for 2002.*

Roman Catholicism

The Vatican is the center of the Roman Catholic Church, and millions of Catholics come to Rome every year to visit there. Most come to see the pope, either at the balcony of his Vatican apartments where he appears most Sundays at noon or at one of his weekly audiences. These audiences are held in a special hall in the Vatican and are attended by eight thousand people at a time. The Roman people themselves, however, are not necessarily churchgoers, and while most Romans claim to be Roman Catholics, only about 10 percent go to Mass regularly.

▼ *After World War II, Rome's population increased. More people moved to the city because the expansion of government departments created more jobs there, while agricultural work became less important.*

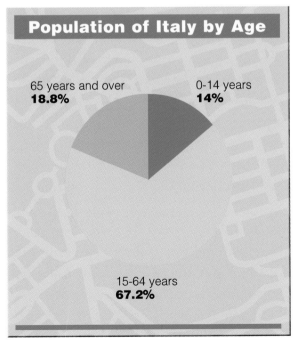

Population of Italy by Age

65 years and over **18.8%**

0-14 years **14%**

15-64 years **67.2%**

Source: Census 2002 – from nationmaster.com/encyclopedia/Demographics-of-Italy

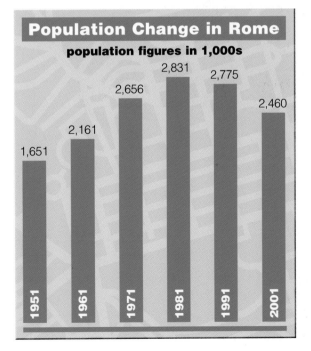

Population Change in Rome

population figures in 1,000s

Year	Population
1951	1,651
1961	2,161
1971	2,656
1981	2,831
1991	2,775
2001	2,460

There are churches for the Anglican, Baptist, Greek and Russian Orthodox, Lutheran, Methodist, and Presbyterian faiths. There is also a Mormon church.

Jews in Rome

There have been Jews in Rome for more than two thousand years, making its Jewish community the oldest in Europe. In 1556, Pope Paul IV ordered that all Jews should live in a walled-off area that became known as the Ghetto. He also imposed curfews on the Jews (orders for them to return home before a certain time), restricted their trading rights, and forced them occasionally to attend Catholic services. The Ghetto was in a particularly unhealthy part of the city, and it soon became squalid and overcrowded, with more than five thousand inhabitants.

In 1848, the people of Rome knocked down the Ghetto walls, and, in 1870, the Jews also regained the full civil rights they had lost in the sixteenth century. During the German occupation of World War II, however, roughly one-quarter of Rome's Jews died in Nazi concentration camps. Many of the survivors owed their lives to the protection of the Roman people.

Today, the community of Jews in Rome numbers about fifteen thousand. Some Jews still live in the Ghetto area, which remains the center of Jewish life in the city, and where the main synagogue is found. The Sinagoga Ebraica stands on Lungotevere, near the Tiber River, and it

▲ A street in Rome's Jewish quarter. This area is home to Europe's oldest Jewish community.

For Roman Catholics, there are hundreds of churches to choose from in Rome. The city also has many places where followers of other forms of Christianity can worship.

◀ Beneath the dome of Saint Peter's Basilica in the Vatican, an ornate canopy designed by Bernini rises above the papal altar. It is believed that the body of Saint Peter was buried on this spot.

also contains a museum of Jewish history. A bomb exploded in the building in the early 1980s, and since then it has been tightly guarded. There are more than a dozen other synagogues in Rome.

"My visit to the Catacombs was not much of a success. I had hardly taken a step into that airless place before I began to feel uncomfortable. . . . "

—Johann Wolfgang von Goethe, German poet and playwright, describing a visit to the catacombs of Rome, *Italian Journey* (1786-1788).

The Catacombs

From the first to the fifth centuries A.D., early Christians buried their dead in underground passages tunneled out of the soft rock beneath Rome. This was because the burial of the dead was forbidden within the city walls and plots for tombs outside the city were expensive. The dead bodies were wrapped in linen cloths and placed on ledges carved out of the walls of the passages. The ledges were sealed with tiles or pieces of marble. In time, the catacombs, as they were called, became places of pilgrimage, as the bones of many saints were buried in them.

Rome's Muslims

Rome is home to a growing community of Muslims. Islam is now the second religion in Rome (after Roman Catholicism) because of the number of Muslim immigrants who have settled in the city. In 1992, Rome's only mosque opened in the Parioli district of Rome. In fact, the Islamic Cultural Center of Rome includes not only a mosque but also an education center, a conference auditorium for four hundred people, and an exhibition area. This spectacular building combines features of traditional Islamic architecture, such as domes, with Western elements.

Festivals and Special Days

Most major holidays in Rome are built round the Christian festivals: Lent, Easter, Christmas, and various saints' days. Romans often leave the city for the public holidays, heading for the beach or the hills. Many residents desert the city during the hot month of August and many stores and businesses close, particularly around the Feast of the Assumption on August 15.

▼ *Huge crowds gather in Saint Peter's Square for the Pope's Easter blessing. Easter is the most important date in the Catholic calendar.*

Snow in August

The Festa della Madonna della Neve *is held, on August 5, in the church of Santa Maria Maggiore. At a time when Rome is baking under the summer sun, this festival celebrates a snowfall. According to legend, in A.D. 352 the Virgin Mary (Jesus's mother) appeared to Pope Liberius in a dream and told him to found a church on a place where he found snow. Miraculously, on August 5, snow fell on the Esquiline Hill. Pope Liberius built Santa Maria Maggiore there, and the legend of the snow is commemorated every year when thousands of flower petals are dropped from the ceiling during a special service in the church.*

The most important of the Christian festivals in Rome is Easter. This is a time when thousands of pilgrims arrive in the city. On Good Friday, there is an evening service led by the pope in the candlelit Colosseum, and, on Easter Sunday, the pope blesses the crowds gathered in Saint Peter's Square and gives his Easter address. Many Romans leave the city on Easter Monday for a picnic, when they traditionally eat Roman pork and *torta pasqualina*—a type of cheese bread served with salami and eggs.

Local Celebrations

Different areas of Rome have their own patron saints and their own local celebrations. During the last two weeks of July, the residents of the Trastevere district celebrate the *Festa di Noantri*. The main street, the Viale Trastevere, is filled with market stalls; there are processions and feasts; and the festival ends with a spectacular fireworks display. Different professions also celebrate their particular saints' days. On May 26, bus drivers celebrate San Filippo Neri, the patron saint of public transportation. On March 19, the feast of Saint Joseph, carpenters traditionally have been given the day off work. This festival is celebrated in the Trionfale area of Rome.

All Romans celebrate the birthday of their city on April 21. The main celebrations are held on the Piazza del Campidoglio on the Aventine Hill. The City Hall (Palazzo Senatorio) and all the other palaces on the hill are lit by Roman candles—short, slow-burning candles. The effect is stunning and the evening is rounded off with fireworks.

Food is Fresh

Rome's colorful and bustling outdoor markets are a daily source of good-quality food. There are few supermarkets in the center of Rome. Instead, many Romans like to shop every day at their local markets and stores to ensure that what they eat is fresh. The best-known markets are held on the Piazza Campo dei Fiori in the centro storico and the Piazza San Cosimato in Trastevere. The market in Piazza Vittorio Emanuele on the Esquiline has an international flavor, with stalls selling food and spices from Asia, Africa, and the Middle East. Throughout the city there are specialty shops where pasta, cured meats, and cheeses can be bought, while bakers offer a wide range of breads and desserts. There are also *kosher* shops that cater to Rome's Jewish community.

Roman Specialties

Cooking and eating are taken very seriously in Rome, both at home and in restaurants. Meals are often very long social occasions. Pasta is a staple of the Italian diet, and one particular pasta dish—*spaghetti alla carbonara* (spaghetti with bacon, cheese, and egg)— was created in Rome. This dish uses Rome's classic cheese *pecorino romano*, which is made from ewe's milk. However, more traditional Roman dishes are based on meat from what is known as the *quinto-quarto* (the "fifth quarter.") This refers to offal—the head, tail, liver, kidneys, and innards of an animal. The use of the quinto-quarto dates from ancient Roman times, when the plebeians were given the leftovers from patrician feasts. Genuine Roman dishes include *tripa alla Romana* (tripe with tomato

▼ *Cured hams hang above the doorways of a specialty food store in the Campo dei Fiori.*

sauce, flavored with mint) and *coratella* (lambs' heart, liver, spleen, and lungs cooked in olive oil).

Romans love to eat pizzas, which are usually rolled very thin and baked in wood-burning stoves. There are also Jewish dishes such as *filetti di baccala* (deep-fried salt cod fillets) and *carciofi fritti* (deep-fried artichokes). Sweet specialties include *maritozzi alla panna*, a soft bun with raisins, pine nuts, and candied fruit, often filled with whipped cream.

International Cuisine

While the vast majority of restaurants in Rome serve Italian food, there is also a good selection of international restaurants, thanks to the city's immigrant population. These include North African restaurants, as well as Chinese, Japanese, Indian, Mexican, and Malaysian. There are also the usual fast-food

▲ *One of the many street cafés in the popular Piazza di Navona where people can eat or just enjoy a drink.*

outlets across the city. Fast food includes places that sell slices of fresh take-out pizza as well as one of the busiest McDonald's in the world, on the Piazza della Repubblica.

Gelaterie and Grattachecche

Ice cream is an important part of everyday life in Rome—particularly in the summer. There are many gelaterie (ice cream parlors) in the city, all offering a vast array of flavors and types of ice cream. The most famous is Giolotti, which was founded in 1900. Ice cream is sold in a cup or a cone and most often comes with whipped cream on top. In the summer, there are also street stands and kiosks that sell grattachecche, delicious shaved ice flavored with fresh fruit.

CHAPTER 3

Living in Rome

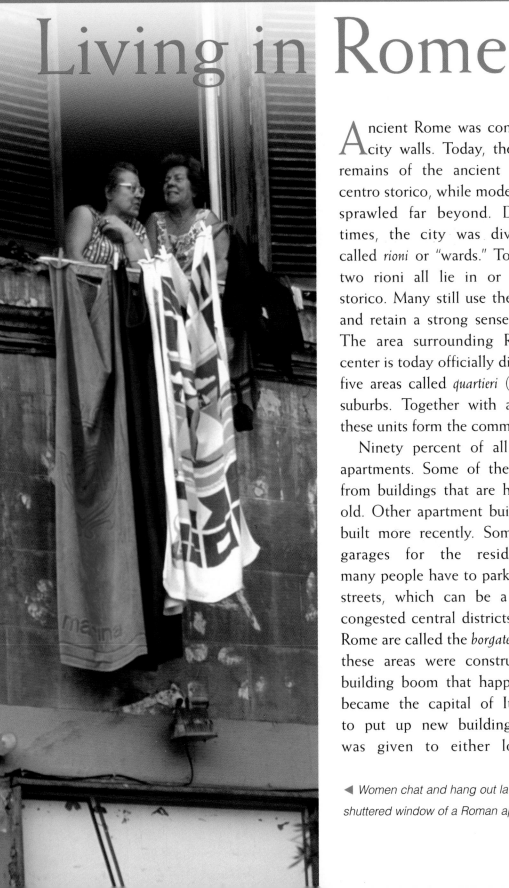

Ancient Rome was contained within its city walls. Today, the area inside the remains of the ancient walls forms the centro storico, while modern-day Rome has sprawled far beyond. During medieval times, the city was divided into areas called *rioni* or "wards." Today, the twenty-two rioni all lie in or near the centro storico. Many still use their ancient names and retain a strong sense of their history. The area surrounding Rome's historical center is today officially divided into thirty-five areas called *quartieri* (quarters) and six suburbs. Together with an outlying area, these units form the commune of Rome.

Ninety percent of all Romans live in apartments. Some of these are converted from buildings that are hundreds of years old. Other apartment buildings have been built more recently. Some of these have garages for the residents' cars, but many people have to park their cars on the streets, which can be a problem in the congested central districts. The suburbs of Rome are called the *borgate,* and a number of these areas were constructed during the building boom that happened after Rome became the capital of Italy. In the rush to put up new buildings, little thought was given to either local services or

◀ *Women chat and hang out laundry at the shuttered window of a Roman apartment.*

Trastevere

The area of Trastevere in the city center lies on the west bank of the Tiber River, south of the Gianicolo Hill. It is one of the most ancient parts of the city, and it was traditionally the main working-class area of Rome. Today the district has a very cosmopolitan feeling. It has thriving Jewish and Indian communities and has become popular with American and British people who are resident in Rome. Full of small craft shops and restaurants, Trastevere attracts many tourists. However, residents can escape the hustle and bustle by visiting one of the many local parks—the Villa Doria Pamphili, the Villa Sciarra, and Rome's Botanical Gardens are all close by.

transportation links to the center city, although initiatives to improve services have been taken more recently.

Green Space

For wealthy residents, there are some beautiful and peaceful residential areas in Rome. Large houses surrounded by gardens line the quiet streets of Parioli, Pinciano, and the Aventine Hill. For the majority, who cannot afford a home with a garden, Rome has a variety of open spaces and parks, some of which are part of large estates, or villas, that were once owned by Rome's

▼ Once an estate owned by the Borghese family, the Villa Borghese is the largest park in central Rome. It has a world-famous art gallery, museums, and a zoo.

wealthiest families. Rome's largest park is the Villa Doria Pamphili, while the most central is the Villa Borghese. The park on the Gianicolo Hill is popular because of the stunning views over the whole city of Rome.

Shopping

In all districts of Rome, there are small specialty shops where the emphasis is on the quality and style of goods. Compared to many other modern cities, Rome has relatively few large department stores and malls, although new ones are opening up, mainly on the outskirts of the city.

"All things are to be bought at Rome."

—Proverb.

▲ *Fresh produce is available daily at market stalls in the Piazza San Cosimato, Trastevere.*

Rome has four major department stores. *La Rinascente* is the most upscale and the only department store in the centro storico. COIN is a mid-range store, while *Standa* and *UPIM* stock inexpensive goods. The *Centro Commerciale* near the Cinecittà film studios has 110 shops, while *La Romanina* and *I Granai* (near EUR) are slightly larger.

Department stores and malls stay open all day, and some open on Sundays, but most smaller shops in Rome still follow traditional opening hours, allowing for a civilized siesta. They usually close for lunch at 1:00 P.M. or 1:30 P.M. and stay closed for the afternoon, only reopening about 4:30 P.M. Most close for the night about 7:30 P.M.

Markets and Street Fairs

In every area of Rome, markets sell fresh food as well as a vast array of other goods. Rome's biggest and best-known flea market (selling antiques and other used goods) is held every Sunday at the Porta Portese in Trastevere. For bargain clothes, Romans go to the daily market (except on Sundays) on Via Sannio in Laterano. Seasonal street fairs also abound. At Christmas time, holiday shoppers can find ornaments and treats at a traditional fair on the Piazza Navona. In the summer, arts and crafts vendors set up stalls along the banks of the river for the Expo Tevere. Antiques fairs are held every year along the two streets that form the center of Rome's antique trade—Via dei Coronari and Via dell'Orso.

Alta Moda

Italy is famous for its alta moda *"high fashion" houses such as* Gucci, Prada, Armani, *and* Versace. *While many fashion designers are based in Milan, they all have stores in Rome. The streets around the Piazza di Spagna, such as the Via dei Condotti* (pictured right), *are filled with designer fashion stores selling clothes at very high prices. Roman fashion designers include Valentino and Laura Biagotti. Valentino set up his studio in 1959 and dressed some of the world's most famous women, including Jacqueline Kennedy. Laura Biagotti has used her wealth to pay for several restoration projects in Rome and has even named a perfume after the city.*

The School System

The majority of children in Italy attend state-run schools, but there are private schools as well. In Rome, many of these private schools are run by religious groups such as the Jesuits. There are also many international schools catering to the large number of people from overseas who work in the city. These provide education for American, British, French, German, Spanish, and Japanese children, among others.

Many children in Rome attend kindergartens, called *scuola materna*, from age three to six. Education is compulsory from the ages of six to fifteen. At six, children go to elementary school, moving to middle school at the age of eleven. High school starts at age fourteen and students leave at the age of nineteen. They must pass the state examination to move on to higher education. There are plans to restructure the

▲ *Children at an elementary school*
in Rome have an English lesson.

school system, abolishing the "middle school" (junior high school), and to extend elementary education to age thirteen. High school education would then last for five years, the first two years being compulsory.

At elementary school, pupils study a broad range of subjects, including reading and writing, a foreign language, math, sciences, history, geography, art, music, and physical education. Roman Catholicism is taught in public schools but is not compulsory. At the end of their fifth year, pupils must take the elementary school examination—a mixture of written and oral tests—which allows them to move on to the middle school. Middle school students follow a similar curriculum, but senior high students are grouped according to subject. They can attend classical and scientific schools to prepare for higher education such as university, or choose more specialized art and music schools, teacher training schools, or other vocational schools.

Higher Education

For those who move on to higher education, there are three state universities in Rome—La Sapienza, Tor Vergata, and Roma Tre. La Sapienza was founded in 1303 by Pope Boniface VIII and is Italy's largest university. There is also a private Italian university, Libera Universita Internazionale degli Studi Sociali (LUISS). A private university is one that is not funded by the state, but has been set up by private individuals and by local associations or foundations. Other private universities are run by different religious orders and international organizations, for example, the American University of Rome and John Cabot University. While these international universities attract students from abroad to live in Rome, most Italian students live at home while they study.

Getting to Rome

Rome has two international airports just outside the city, Leonardo da Vinci—usually called Fiumicino after the town nearby—and Ciampino. Most travelers with scheduled flights use the main airport, Fiumicino. It lies about 19 miles (30 km) southwest of Rome and is linked to the city by a fast train service. Most of those on charter flights fly into Ciampino. It is about 9 miles (15 km) southeast of the city. Together, Rome's airports handled over 26 million passengers in 2002, flying to or from 160 destinations on 120 different airlines.

Rome is linked to the rest of Italy by a network of roads and railroads. The main station in the center of Rome, and the hub of the national train system, is Termini. Trains arrive and depart here to serve all of Italy and other parts of Europe. Trains connecting the city center with the suburbs run from stations such as Porta San Paolo and Roma Nord. The main road route connecting Rome to other Italian cities is the Autostrada del Sole, which links Milan in the north with Reggio di Calabria in the south. The autoroute, or expressway, connects with a beltway that runs around the outskirts of Rome.

Getting About

In Rome itself, the main methods of public transportation are bus, streetcar, the metro system, and local trains that run to the suburbs or towns near Rome. They are all part of the same system, and passengers can use the same ticket on all forms of transportation. A single ticket lasts for seventy-five minutes, but passengers can buy tickets for the day, the week, or the month. Buses and streetcars are painted orange, with some newer streetcars painted green.

The subway, or metro, system is small, with only two lines totalling 25.6 miles (41.2 km) in length. Line A runs from

Black Night?

On the evening of September 27, 2003, Rome held its first official Notte Bianca ("White Night"). This was a night when nothing in the city closed—museums, theaters, galleries, movie theaters, sports centers, and shops stayed open all night. There were also hundreds of special events, and many people were determined to stay up all night and enjoy the fun. Unfortunately, the city was soon gridlocked as people ignored advice to leave their cars at home. Then, at about 3:00 A.M., it started to rain. Half an hour later, the lights went out, and Rome was plunged into darkness. The massive power outage affected most of Italy, and supply lines from France were blamed. When it became clear that the power was not going to return quickly, most Romans made their way home as best they could.

Battistini in the northwest to Anagnina in the southeast. Line B extends from Rebibbia in the northeast to EUR (Laurentina) in the south. The two lines form an X shape and cross at Termini. The size of the metro system has been limited by the number of archaeological remains that lie beneath the city, which cause problems and delays whenever new tunneling work begins.

Rome's Traffic

Traffic is a major problem in Rome. Traffic fills the city's streets, particularly at rush hour times, in the morning, at lunch time, again around 4:00 P.M. when people return to work, and between 7:30 P.M. and 8:00 P.M. at the end of the day. In an effort to control the amount of traffic entering the narrow

▲ *Streetcars in Rome are inexpensive to use. Before boarding, patrons buy tickets from stores or machines.*

streets of the city center, the city council has tried out various plans. One plan was to allow vehicles with number plates ending with odd numbers and even numbers to enter a restricted zone on alternate days. Many Romans got around that by buying a second car and so it was quietly dropped. Now the city council has introduced a permit plan, which allows only vehicles with a permit to enter the restricted area in the city center.

Traffic congestion is more than just a nuisance. Traffic is responsible for 85 percent of the air pollution in Rome. This air pollution and also the vibration caused by the traffic is doing some serious damage to ancient monuments across the city, such as the Colosseum. Some squares and streets in the historical center of the city are now pedestrian-only zones.

Clean-up Operation

The Vatican declared the year 2000 a Holy Year for the Roman Catholic Church, and it is estimated that 25 million pilgrims made their way to Rome in that year. In anticipation of this massive influx of people and in an effort to modernize Rome, the city council spent several years and a lot of money cleaning buildings and improving Rome's infrastructure. Many blackened buildings were shrouded in scaffolding, only to reappear a few months later, bright and

"Cars, taxis, buses, and motor scooters all went plunging at once down the narrow length of it [the street] or swerving perilously around a fountain."

—Elizabeth Spencer, American author, describing Rome's traffic, *The White Azalea*, 1961.

clean. To help move traffic, a new underpass was built to ease congestion near Saint Peter's Square. Streetcar lines have been built or extended, and plans to construct new metro lines are going forward.

▼ *A traffic officer directs the flow of traffic in the Via del Corso, one of Rome's main shopping streets.*

CHAPTER 4

Rome at Work

Rome's economy is largely based on two areas: tourism and government administration. The city is also home to several United Nations agencies, including the United Nations Food and Agriculture Organization (FAO), the International Fund for Agricultural Development (IFAD), and the World Food Program.

Although Rome is Italy's capital city, it is not the Italian center of finance and industry. Italy's financial center, including the main stock exchange, is in the northern city of Milan. Rome has its own stock exchange, the Roma Borsa, but it is less important, and Roman stockbrokers use the internet to access the main center in Milan. Similarly, the northern cities of Milan, Turin, and Genoa are the centers of heavy industry, such as steel and car production. In fact, after World War II, the development of heavy industry in Rome was discouraged by the government. Instead, light industries such as pharmaceuticals, printing, and textiles were set up in the main industrial areas in the northwest of the city.

The Roman Workforce

A large percentage of the city's workforce is employed by the national and city governments, by agencies such as those run

◄ *A worker checks the quality of the dry spaghetti produced by machine in a Roman factory.*

Cinecittà

Movie-making has been an important industry in Rome since the 1930s. In 1937, a huge movie studio, Cinecittà, was set up in the south of the city. This was one of Mussolini's grand projects, and under the Fascists, propaganda films were made to glorify the Italian state. Later, it was here that Italian directors such as Roberto Rossellini and Federico Fellini made classic films such as Roma Città Aperta (Rome, Open City) *and* La Dolce Vita (The Good Life). *Hollywood blockbusters of the 1950s and 1960s, such as* Quo Vadis? Ben Hur, *and* Cleopatra *were also made at Cinecittà. Today, the studio continues to be an important and thriving center for the Italian film industry. The picture above shows the producer and director of the 1999 movie* Tea with Mussolini *at work in the Cinecittà Studios.*

by the United Nations, and by the tourist industry. Other main employers include the service industries such as banking, insurance, and the retail trade. Rome is also Italy's leading center for high-tech industries such as computer engineering and public communications. Since Rome is the center of the Roman Catholic Church, the Vatican's administrative offices also employ many Romans.

The working day in Rome begins about 8:30 to 9 :00 A.M. The traditional lunch break is long, from 1:00 or 1:30 P.M. to 3:00 or 4:00 P.M., and people are accustomed to going home for lunch and a siesta or going to a restaurant. Their working day ends at 7:00 or 8:00 P.M. Now, however, many offices work *orario nonstop* (open all day), with only a short break for lunch. Some offices and businesses shut completely for August, as most Romans take their summer vacation out of the city.

National Government

Italy is divided into *regioni* (regions), *provinci* (provinces), and *comuni* (municipalities). The Comune di Roma (Commune of Rome) lies in the province of Rome, which is one of the five provinces that make up the Lazio region. Ever since Rome became the capital of Italy in 1871, it has been the seat of national government in Italy. Italy is a parliamentary republic, headed by a president. Its parliament has two houses—a Senate with 315 members and a Chamber of

▲ *Statues grace the Piazza del Campidoglio and the Palazzo Senatorio (center), Rome's city hall.*

Deputies with 630 members. This modern government resides in buildings steeped in history: The president's official residence is the Palazzo del Quirinale (former summer residence of the Pope). The Chamber of Deputies meets in the Palazzo di Montecitorio. The Senate meets in the Palazzo Madama, a sixteenth century palace built for the powerful Medici family.

Mani Pulite

In 1992, investigations called mani pulite *("clean hands") were started by a magistrate in Milan. These investigations looked at allegations that large bribes were being paid by businesses to Italian politicians. During the 1990s, hundreds of people were investigated, including Italian politicians at all levels of government and many business people in Rome and elsewhere. The investigations even extended to Silvio Berlusconi, now prime minister of Italy. Mani pulite continues today, in an effort to create a more honest system of government and business in Italy.*

◀ *Francesco Rutelli at an election rally in Rome, 2001. Elected mayor of Rome in 1993, then again in 1997, Rutelli oversaw extensive preparations for the expected arrival of millions of pilgrims to the city in the jubilee year of 2000.*

Municipal Government

Rome's city council is based on the Capitoline Hill. The seat of government during Ancient Roman times, it has remained the home of the municipal government ever since. The city council meets in the City Hall—the Palazzo Senatorio—one of the beautiful buildings around the Piazza del Campidoglio that were designed by Michelangelo.

The city council has a mayor (*sindaco*) who is elected every four years by the Roman public. The mayor appoints ministers to run different city departments. These ministers are drawn from the council itself, a group of elected officials. In 2001, Walter Veltroni took over from Francesco Rutelli as Rome's mayor. A former deputy prime minister and Minister for Cultural Heritage, Walter Veltroni has had a distinguished career as a national politician.

CHAPTER 5

Rome at Play

Rome offers a wide variety of entertainment. Many concerts and movie showings take place in the open air, and during the summer there are a variety of cultural festivals and events held throughout the city. Discos, clubs, and—a new addition to the entertainment scene — pubs are very popular with tourists and residents alike. Romans can find out what's happening in their city by looking in such weekly listings magazines as *Citta Apertà* and *Roma C'è*.

Sport

The most popular sport in Rome is soccer. Romans have two soccer teams to choose from: AS Roma and Lazio. Both play in Serie A—the top division of the Italian soccer league—and the teams share the Olympic Stadium. Basketball and tennis are also popular sports, and the Italian International Tennis Championships are held every May on clay courts in the Foro Italico, a sports complex in a northwest suburb of Rome. In the same month, an international horse show is held in the Piazza di Siena, an arena set in the beautiful parkland of the Villa Borghese.

◀ *Fans celebrate a victory of Rome's soccer team, AS Roma, with a concert in the Circus Maximus. In the fourth century B.C. this was the largest of the Ancient Roman arenas, where huge crowds would gather to watch chariot racing.*

Roma versus Lazio

Soccer is a passion for many Romans, and one of the most anticipated events in the sporting calendar is a clash between the two local teams AS Roma and Lazio. AS Roma supporters are known as romanisti, and traditionally come from working-class areas of Rome such as Trastevere. Lazio supporters traditionally come from areas around Rome. In the Stadio Olimpico, Roma fans occupy the Curva Sud (south end), while Lazio fans sit in the Curva Nord (north end).

▲ *Visitors wind down the spiral staircase at the entrance to the Vatican Museums. This vast museum complex has more than 5 miles (8 km) of corridors.*

Museums and Galleries

The city has a wealth of museums and galleries that contain some of the world's most important works of art. The best-known include the Vatican Museums and the museums on the Capitoline Hill. The National Museum of Rome has a huge collection of archaeological finds from sites across the city. Other museums are in the former palaces of wealthy families such as the Palazzo Corsini and the Palazzo Barberini. Here, you can see the fabulous collections of works of art that were acquired by these families during the Renaissance and Baroque periods.

Music, Theater, and Dance

Concerts and opera take place in all types of venues, from theaters and concert halls to churches, gardens, and ancient ruins. Rome's new Music Park opened in 2002, and Rome's Santa Cecilia Orchestra is just one of the groups that perform there regularly. Opera is a popular spectacle in Italy, and although Rome's opera is not as prestigious as that of Milan's great opera house, La Scala,

Parco della Musica

This new "Music Park" opened in 2002 and is the largest music complex in Italy. It stands between the Olympic Village and the Palazzetto dello Sport in the north of Rome. It was designed by the Italian architect Renzo Piano, and work started on the project in 1996. Construction was held up, however, by the discovery of the remains of a Roman villa on the site. While the villa was being excavated, Piano revised his designs to include the remains. The Music Park includes three separate concert halls, one holding 2,800 people, another for 1,200 people, and a small hall that seats 700. The halls are designed to accommodate all types of music from classical concerts to folk and rock. The Music Park is run by Rome's Santa Cecilia Music Conservatory.

productions at the Teatro dell'Opera always draw large crowds. In the summer, opera is performed outdoors at the Stadio Olimpico (Olympic Stadium) in northern Rome, built for the 1960 Olympic Games, and occasionally at the ruins of the ancient Roman Baths of Caracalla on the Celio Hill. There is no specific venue for big rock concerts in Rome, but rock fans often enjoy performances at the Palazzo dello Sport in EUR and at various other stadiums.

There are more than eighty theaters in Rome, but the Teatro Argentina is the official home of the Teatro di Roma, Rome's state-funded theater company. Many theatrical performances are staged outdoors in the summer, in venues such as the Anfiteatro Quercia del Tasso, an ancient amphitheater in the park on the Gianicolo Hill. Dance lovers can see occasional productions at the Teatro dell'Opera as well as at the Teatro Olimpico. There are more than eighty movie theaters in Rome, and an international film festival takes place on the Isola Tiberina (Tiber Island) during the summer. Some movie theaters have roofs that can be rolled back for open-air viewing on hot summer evenings.

Summer and Fall Festivals

There are many big summer and fall festivals in Rome. The Estata Romana is sponsored and promoted by the city government and brings together many different events from June through September. In the months of October and

▲ *The mountain ranges of the Lazio region offer escape from the noise and bustle of Rome.*

November, *RomaEuropa* is the big festival, featuring opera, dance, and music from all over the world. At the same time, the Roma Jazz Festival attracts top international jazz performers to its venues, which include the Auditorium Massimo in EUR and *Alexanderplatz*, Rome's leading jazz club.

Getting Away

When Romans want to escape their city, they head to the beaches at Ostia and Anzio farther south. The lakes of northern Lazio are another popular destination. Many wealthy Romans have weekend and vacation homes in the Lazio countryside. In the winter, it is possible to ski in a few of the higher parts of the Lazio hills.

CHAPTER 6

Looking Forward

Part of Rome's fascination for visitor and resident alike is its exciting mixture of ancient and ultra-modern. New metro lines must be routed to avoid priceless archaeological remains; performances of modern plays and music are given against backdrops of ancient ruins; cars and scooters weave in and out around buildings that are thousands of years old. Tourists flock to Rome to see its heritage, yet they also expect all the amenities of a twenty-first-century city.

One plan for Rome intends to undo some of the damage caused to its archaeological heritage by the Fascists. When Mussolini ordered the construction of the Via dei Fori Imperiali, the new road covered up large parts of the ancient Roman forum. There are now plans to remove the Via dei Fori Imperiali and to create in its place a large archaeological site to uncover the full extent of the forum. More controversial is the idea of Professor Carlo Aymonino, a former professor of architecture in Rome, to "improve" the Colosseum by filling in the gaps in the outside walls with bricks. This plan has led to horrified reactions from many scholars and architects, but

◀ *Striking modern architecture holds a place within the Eternal City. This auditorium is part of the Parco della Musica complex designed by Italian architect Renzo Piano.*

Rome's Globe Theater

In October, 2003, Rome's very own Globe Theater opened its doors for the first time. This is a replica of the Globe Theater in London, where the plays of William Shakespeare were first performed four hundred years ago. The theater is built from wood and is open to the sky—just like the original. It was constructed in only four months in the park of the Villa Borghese in Rome. Its opening night was marked by a performance in Italian of Shakespeare's play Romeo and Juliet, although it will be used for a wide variety of theatrical and musical performances.

▲ Computer technology was used in the restoration of Michelangelo's frescos. Caring for Rome's heritage is an important and expensive business.

Professor Aymonino believes that there is a strong case for completing buildings when there is evidence that shows how they originally looked.

Improving Communications

The problems of bringing this ancient city up-to-date and into the twenty-first century were first tackled in the 1990s by the Roman mayor, Francesco Rutelli. A delicate balance needs to be struck between preserving a huge array of ancient monuments and priceless art and architecture, while transforming Rome into a modern city with modern communications.

One project to update the city has involved laying underground fiber optic cables. These cables have modernized the city's telephone network. Another modernizing project that has been many years in the making is the extension of the city's subway. It has been complicated by the fact that new lines have to avoid the monuments and the archaeological remains that lie beneath the city's surface. Plans to build a new line C and to extend line B are finally going ahead, however. A branch line off Line B will head northward to Conca d'Oro. A new section of line will run beneath the city center to the Vatican and then northward. Once completed, Line C will be 19 miles (30 km) long and have thirty-five stations. Combining modern travel and communications with access to the priceless history of its city, Rome is heading into the future with optimism—while keeping its past intact.

Time Line

753 B.C. Legendary date of the foundation of Rome.

616 B.C. Beginning of the rule of Etruscan king, Tarquinius.

509 B.C. Romans overthrow the Etruscans and the Roman Republic begins.

494 B.C. Tribunes are elected to the Senate and the Twelve Tables provide the republic with a legal framework.

146 B.C. The Punic Wars come to an end.

27 B.C. The Roman Republic comes to an end and Augustus becomes the first Roman emperor.

A.D. 64 Much of Rome is destroyed by fire.

313 Christians are allowed to worship freely in Rome.

410 The Visigoths sack Rome.

455 The Vandals sack Rome.

476 The western part of Roman Empire collapses.

1303 Pope Boniface VIII founds University of Rome.

1309 Pope Clement V abandons Rome for Avignon, France.

1377 The Pope returns to Rome.

1527 The army of Charles V of Spain sacks Rome.

1556 Jews are confined to the Ghetto in Rome.

1797 Napoleon sacks Rome.

1798 Napoleon declares the new Roman Republic.

1801–1808 Rome is again under papal rule, but this ends when Napoleon removes the pope.

1814 Papal rule is re-established following Napoleon's defeat.

1861 The Kingdom of Italy is founded with capital at Turin.

1871 Rome becomes the capital of a unified Italy.

1922 Mussolini's troops, the "black shirts," march on Rome.

1929 The Lateran Treaty establishes the Vatican City as a separate state.

1937 Opening of the Cinecittà movie studio.

1940 Italy enters World War II.

1943 Rome is occupied by the Germans and declared an "open city."

1944 The German occupation of Rome comes to an end.

1945 Mussolini is executed.

1946 Italians vote for their country to become a republic.

1957 Treaty of Rome begins European Community.

1960 The Olympic Games are held in Rome.

1990 Rome hosts the soccer World Cup.

2000 Jubilee "Holy Year" is celebrated in Rome, attracting millions of pilgrims.

2001 The lira is replaced by the euro, which can be used as common currency in a number of European countries.

Glossary

Allies during World War II, countries (including Great Britain, the United States, and France) that fought against Germany and the other "Axis" powers.

apostle the term used to describe the twelve chosen followers (disciples) of Jesus Christ.

autoroute an expressway.

Baroque the name describing art, architecture, and music in the period from roughly 1600 to the middle of the eighteenth century.

basilica a type of early Christian church, modeled on large Roman halls used for administrative and judicial purposes.

catacombs underground burial tunnels.

centro storico (historical center) the center of Rome, marked by the ancient city walls.

Colosseum the largest outdoor theater in ancient Rome. Its ruins stand today in the center of Rome.

consul the highest office in the Roman Republic. There were two consuls, elected each year.

Counter-Reformation a movement of reform in the Catholic Church which was started mainly as a result of the Protestant Reformation.

Etruscans a tribe who lived in central Italy (Etruria) from the middle of the ninth century. They controlled Rome until 509 B.C.

Fascism a movement that was founded in 1921 by Benito Mussolini in Italy. One of its main features is rule by a dictator.

fiber optic describes glass fibers used to transmit data.

forum the area of an Ancient Roman town or city that was its administrative, business, and social center.

ghetto a section of a city inhabited by people of a minority group. In Rome, the Ghetto is the Jewish quarter of the city.

Jesuits describes members of a religious order called the Society of Jesus, which was founded in 1540 by Ignatius de Loyola.

kosher food that is prepared according to Jewish law.

Lent in the Christian calendar, the weeks leading up to Easter. It begins on Ash Wednesday.

Mass the main service of the Roman Catholic Church.

Medieval the name given to describe the period known as the Middle Ages that occurred between the fall of the Roman Empire (476) and the Renaissance (approximately 1450).

patrician describes members of aristocratic families in ancient Rome.

plebeian describes the ordinary people of ancient Rome.

pope the Bishop of Rome, also the head of the Roman Catholic Church.

Protestant the term used to describe those Christians who broke away from the Catholic Church during the Reformation, as well as the churches they set up.

referendum a vote by the electorate on a specific issue.

Reformation a protest movement for the reform of the Roman Catholic Church, sparked by Martin Luther in 1517.

Renaissance (from the French, meaning "re-birth") the term given to a period, from roughly 1450–1600, when classical literature and the arts inspired a revival in culture and learning in Europe.

republic a form of government with leaders who are elected.

Risorgimento ("Resurgence" or "Rebirth") the movement (1815–1870) for the unification of the many small states and kingdoms that existed in Italy.

Senate the council that advised the consuls in Republican Rome.

stock exchange a place where stocks, shares, and securities are bought and sold.

tribunes representatives of the plebeians in the Senate in ancient Rome.

Further Information

Books

Biesty, Stephen, and Andrew Solway, *Rome: In Spectacular Cross Section*. Scholastic, 2003.

Bingham, Jane, *The Usborne Encyclopedia of the Roman World: Internet-Linked*. Usborne Publishing 2002.

Corbishley, Mike, *Illustrated Encyclopedia of Ancient Rome*. J. Paul Getty Museum Publications, 2004.

Hibbert, Christopher, *Rome: The Biography of a City*. Penguin USA, 1988.

McKeever, Susan, *DK Pockets: Ancient Rome*. Dorling Kindersley, 1995.

Rome Insight Guide. APA Publications, 2003.

Web Sites

en.wikipedia.org/wiki/Rome
Find out more about Rome, its history, and Latin.

www.frommers.com/destinations/rome/006 4020048.html
Read about walking tours and highlights of Rome:

www.historylink101.com/ancient_ rome.htm
Discover ancient Roman art, daily life, and more.

members.aol.com/Donnclass/Romelife.html
Learn about daily life in Ancient Rome.

mp_pollett.tripod.com/rioni.htm
Explore many of Rome's districts and landmarks.

Index

Page numbers in **bold** indicate pictures.